Summary

Chapter 1: Introduction to Predictive Analytics with C# and ML.NET

Machine Learning Basics: The Magic Behind Artificial Intelligence

Imagine a world where machines can learn and make decisions almost like us humans. Well, you don't have to imagine much, because this world is already here! It's the fascinating universe of Machine Learning (ML).

What is Machine Learning, anyway?

Machine learning is like teaching a computer to fish, rather than giving it the fish. Instead of programming specific rules for each situation, we allow the computer to learn from data and experience, improving its decisions over time.

The Three Musketeers of ML

ML generally falls into three main approaches:

- **Supervised Learning:** It's like learning from a teacher. We provide labeled data (the correct answers) and the model learns to make predictions for new data.
- **Unsupervised Learning:** Here, the model is like a detective, looking for patterns in unlabeled data. It groups similar information together without knowing the categories beforehand.
- **Reinforcement Learning:** Think of it like training a dog. The model learns through trial and error, receiving rewards for correct actions and penalties for mistakes.

Why is ML so powerful?

ML shines where traditional rules fail. It can:

- Recognize complex patterns in large volumes of data
- Adapt to new information without reprogramming
- Automate tasks that previously required human intelligence

You probably use ML more than you realize:

- Email spam filters
- Netflix or Spotify recommendations
- Virtual assistants like Siri or Alexa
- Fraud detection in banking transactions

The Heart of ML: Algorithms and Data

ML algorithms are like cake recipes, each with its own specific purpose. Some popular ones include:

- Decision Trees
- Neural Networks
- K-Means for clustering
- Linear Regression

But remember: an algorithm is only as good as the data it's powered by. Quality data is the fuel that makes the magic of ML happen.

Machine learning isn't just a technology; it's a new way of thinking about problems and solutions. Whether you're a beginner or an experienced programmer, diving into ML opens up a world of exciting possibilities. So why not take the first step on this journey? The future is waiting for you!

The Power of Prediction: Why Predictive Analytics Matters

Imagine if you could predict the future. Sounds like science fiction, right? Well, with predictive analytics, we can get pretty close! Predictive analytics uses data from the past and present to make predictions about the future. It's like having a digital crystal ball!

In business, this could mean predicting which customers are most likely to cancel a service, which product will be the next best-seller, or even when a machine might break down before it happens. Cool, huh?

And the best part? You can do all this using C# and ML.NET. Let's dive into this fascinating world!

All examples given in this ebook were made in Visual Studio 2022 and are available at https://github.com/wagnersalvi/LivroMaquinas

ML.NET: Your New Best Friend

ML.NET is like that nerdy friend who always has the answer to everything. It's a machine learning library created by Microsoft specifically for .NET developers. With it, you can add artificial intelligence to your C# applications without needing to be a math genius or a PhD in data science.

Installing the ML.Net library

To install the ML.NET library in Visual Studio and start using it, follow these steps:

- Open your project in Visual Studio.
- Right-click the project name in Solution Explorer.
- Select "Manage NuGet Packages".
- In the "Browse" tab, search for "Microsoft.ML".
- Select the "Microsoft.ML" package and click "Install".
- Accept the license terms and wait for the installation.

Additionally, you can install the ML.NET Model Builder, which is a Visual Studio extension that makes building models easier:

- In Visual Studio, go to "Extensions" > "Manage Extensions".
- Search for "ML.NET Model Builder".
- Click "Download" and follow the instructions to install.

ML.NET is a powerful library that lets you add machine learning capabilities to your .NET applications. Some of its key features include:

- Binary and multiclass classification: Categorize data into two or more classes.
- Regression: Predicting continuous numerical values.
- Anomaly detection: Identify unusual patterns in data.
- Recommendation: Create product or item recommendation systems.
- Clustering: Grouping similar data together.
- Natural language processing: Sentiment analysis, text classification, etc.
- Time series forecasting: Making predictions based on historical data.
- Computer vision: Image classification, object detection.
- AutoML: Automate the process of model selection and training.
- Integration with other frameworks: Work with models from TensorFlow, ONNX, etc.
- Local training and inference: Train and use models without the need for an internet connection.
- Model evaluation: Metrics to evaluate the performance of trained models.

With ML.NET, you can build intelligent applications in C# or F#, leveraging your existing .NET skills to implement machine learning solutions in a variety of scenarios, from sentiment analysis to price prediction, fraud detection, and more.

Getting your hands dirty with ML.Net

Want an example of how easy it is to use the ML.Net library? Here's how simple it is to create a basic forecasting model:

```
var mlContext = new MLContext();
var                     model                     =
mlContext.Regression.Trainers.Sdca();

var trainedModel = model.Fit(trainData);
var                  predictions                  =
trainedModel.Transform(testData);
```

Don't worry if this seems a little confusing right now. We'll unravel each part as we go through the book!

Your First Model: Predicting House Prices

Let's get started and create our first predictive model. Imagine you work for a real estate agency and want to predict the price of houses based on a few characteristics.

First, let's define our data:

```
14 referências
public class DadosImovel
{
    [LoadColumn(0)]
    10 referências
    public float Tamanho { get; set; }

    [LoadColumn(1)]
    0 referências
    public float Quartos { get; set; }

    [LoadColumn(2)]
    8 referências
    public float Preco { get; set; }
}

1 referência
public class PredicaoImovel
{
    [ColumnName("Score")]
    1 referência
    public float PrecoPrevisao { get; set; }
}
```

Now, let's create and train our model:

```
MLContext contextoML = new MLContext();

// 1. Importar ou criar dados de treinamento
DadosImovel[] dadosCasas = new DadosImovel[]
{
    new DadosImovel { Tamanho = 110.0F, Preco = 120.0F },
    new DadosImovel { Tamanho = 190.0F, Preco = 230.0F },
    new DadosImovel { Tamanho = 280.0F, Preco = 300.0F },
    new DadosImovel { Tamanho = 340.0F, Preco = 370.0F }
};
IDataView dadosTreinamento = contextoML.Data.LoadFromEnumerable(dadosCasas);

// 2. Especificar pipeline de preparação de dados e treinamento do modelo
var pipeline = contextoML.Transforms.Concatenate("Features", new[] { "Tamanho" })
    .Append(contextoML.Regression.Trainers.Sdca(labelColumnName: "Preco",
        maximumNumberOfIterations: 100));

// 3. Treinar modelo
var modelo = pipeline.Fit(dadosTreinamento);
```

You've just created your first machine learning model in C#. It wasn't that hard, was it?

Testing Our Model: Does It Work?

Now that we have our model, let's see if it actually works:

```
// 4. Fazer uma previsão
var motorPrevisao = contextoML.Model.CreatePredictionEngine<DadosImovel, PredicaoImovel>(modelo);

var tamanhoParaPrever = new DadosImovel { Tamanho = 200.0F };
var previsaoPreco = motorPrevisao.Predict(tamanhoParaPrever);

Console.WriteLine($"Preço previsto para tamanho: {tamanhoParaPrever.Tamanho} " +
    $"m² = R${previsaoPreco.PrecoPrevisao * 1000:F2}k");
```

Evaluating model quality

An important step in any data analysis is to assess the quality of the model, so this assessment is being done below.

```
// 5. Avaliar modelo
DadosImovel[] dadosTesteCasas = new DadosImovel[]
{
    new DadosImovel { Tamanho = 110.0F, Preco = 98.0F },
    new DadosImovel { Tamanho = 190.0F, Preco = 210.0F },
    new DadosImovel { Tamanho = 280.0F, Preco = 290.0F },
    new DadosImovel { Tamanho = 340.0F, Preco = 360.0F }
};
var dadosTesteCasasView = contextoML.Data.LoadFromEnumerable(dadosTesteCasas);
var dadosPrecoTeste = modelo.Transform(dadosTesteCasasView);
var metricas = contextoML.Regression.Evaluate(dadosPrecoTeste, labelColumnName: "Preco");

Console.WriteLine($"R²: {metricas.RSquared:F2}");
Console.WriteLine($"Erro RMS: {metricas.RootMeanSquaredError:F2}");
```

Code Explanation

Initial Configuration

- Machine Learning Context: Launches a new ML context (MLContext) that serves as the entry point to ML.NET.

Training Dataset

- Defines an array of PropertyData with property size and price data.
- Load this data into an IDataView, which is ML.NET's input format for data pipelines.

Data Visualization

- Converts the data back to an enumerable list to review in the console, confirming that the data was loaded correctly.

Model Preparation and Training Pipeline

- Replacing Missing Values: Initializes the data transformation pipeline by replacing missing values in columns with the mean (although there are no missing values here at first).
- Concatenate Features: Concatenates features (other data columns) to be used for training into a "Features" column.
- Model Training: Selects the "Sdca" (Stochastic Dual Coordinate Ascent) algorithm for regression, which will attempt to learn to predict the price from the training data.

Model Training

- Fits (trains) the model with the full pipeline on the loaded training data.

Prediction

- Creates an ML.NET PredictionEngine that allows you to predict new input data.
- Performs a price forecast for a new property with a specified size (200 m^2) and prints the result.

Model Evaluation

- Define a separate test set to evaluate the accuracy of the model.
- Transforms test data using the trained model and calculates quantitative evaluation metrics (R^2 and RMS) to analyze model performance.
- R^2 (Coefficient of determination) measures the efficiency of the model, and the Root Mean Square Error (RMS) indicates the accuracy of the predictions.

A quick explanation about Quality Assessment

R^2 (R-squared) and RMS (Root Mean Square) error are two important metrics used to evaluate the performance of regression models. Let's explain each of them:

R^2 (R-squared)

R^2 is a statistical measure that represents the proportion of variance in the dependent variable that is predictable from the independent variables.

Main features:

- It varies between 0 and 1 (or 0% to 100%).
- The closer to 1, the better the model fits the data.
- Also known as coefficient of determination.

Interpretation:

- An R^2 of 0.7 means that 70% of the variability in the data is explained by the model.
- An R^2 of 1 indicates that the model explains 100% of the variability in the data.

Limitations:

- It does not indicate whether the model is adequate or whether the predictions are biased.
- It can be artificially inflated by adding more variables, even if they are not relevant.

RMS Error (Root Mean Square Error)

RMS error is a measure of the average magnitude of model prediction errors.

Main features:

- Expressed in the same unit as the dependent variable.
- Always positive.
- The smaller the value, the better the model fit.

Calculation:

- The difference between each predicted and observed value is calculated.
- Square each difference.
- The average of these squares is calculated.
- The square root of this average is extracted.

Interpretation:

- Represents the standard deviation of the residuals (prediction errors).
- Useful for understanding the typical magnitude of model errors.

Advantages:

- Penalizes larger errors more heavily than smaller errors.
- Easily interpretable, as it is on the same scale as the dependent variable.
- Both metrics are complementary and provide different insights into model performance. R^2 gives an idea of the overall goodness of fit, while RMS error provides a measure of the magnitude of prediction errors.

If everything goes well, you'll see a price prediction for the test home. Magic? No, just data science!

What's Next?

This is just the beginning of our journey into the world of predictive analytics with C#. In the next chapters, we will explore:

- How to prepare your data for best results
- Different types of models for different problems
- How to evaluate and improve the accuracy of your model
- Advanced techniques for dealing with real-world data

Ready to continue this adventure? Let's go!

Chapter 2: Fundamentals of Data Preprocessing

Let's dive into the fascinating world of data preparation for machine learning, using house price prediction as an example. Imagine yourself as a digital architect, building not just houses, but powerful predictive models. We'll explore the three crucial steps of this process: data loading and visualization, data cleaning and transformation, and the alchemy of feature engineering. All using the magic of ML.NET!

Data Loading and Visualization

Loading data is the first crucial step in any machine learning project. It's like opening the door to the world of information your model will learn.

In ML.NET, data loading is simplified through the use of IDataView. Let's see how this is done in our house prices example:

```csharp
MLContext contextoML = new MLContext();

// 1. Importar ou criar dados de treinamento
DadosImovel[] dadosCasas = new DadosImovel[]
{
    new DadosImovel { Tamanho = 110.0F, Preco = 120.0F },
    new DadosImovel { Tamanho = 190.0F, Preco = 230.0F },
    new DadosImovel { Tamanho = 280.0F, Preco = 300.0F },
    new DadosImovel { Tamanho = 340.0F, Preco = 370.0F }
};
IDataView dadosTreinamento = contextoML.Data.LoadFromEnumerable(dadosCasas);
```

This code loads our data into an IDataView, which is a versatile and efficient representation of data in ML.NET. It's like creating a virtual table that ML.NET can easily manipulate and process.

Although ML.NET does not provide built-in visualization tools, visualizing data is crucial to understanding its characteristics. We can use external libraries or simply print the data for an initial inspection:

```
var preview = contextoML.Data.CreateEnumerable<DadosImovel>(dadosTreinamento, reuseRowObject: false);
foreach (var casa in preview)
{
    Console.WriteLine($"Tamanho: {casa.Tamanho} m², Preço: R${casa.Preco}k");
}
```

This visualization helps us identify patterns, outliers, and relationships between variables, which are crucial for the next steps.

Data Cleansing and Transformation

Data cleaning and transformation are like polishing a rough diamond. They prepare the data to be used efficiently by the machine learning model.

Although our example is simple and does not require extensive cleaning, in real cases we might deal with missing values or outliers:

```
var pipeline = mlContext.Transforms.ReplaceMissingValues(
    outputColumnName: "TamanhoProcessado",
    inputColumnName: "Tamanho",
    replacementMode: MissingValueReplacingEstimator.ReplacementMode.Mean);
```

In this example:

- outputColumnName: This is the name of the new column that will be created with the replaced values.
- inputColumnName: This is the name of the original column that contains the missing values.
- replacementMode: Defines how missing values will be replaced.

ReplacementMode is an enum that offers several options:

- Mean: Replaces with the mean of the non-missing values.
- Median: Replaces with the median of the non-missing values.
- Mode: Replaces with the most frequent value (mode).
- DefaultValue: Replaces with a default value (0 for numeric, empty string for text, etc.).

For example above This pipeline will create a new column called "ProcessedSize" where the missing values from the "Size" column will be replaced by the average of the non-missing values.

Feature Engineering

Feature engineering is where creativity meets data. It is the process of creating new features or modifying existing ones to improve model performance.

In our house price example, we could create a new feature that represents the price per square meter:

```
var pipeline = contextoML.Transforms.Expression(
    "PrecoM2",
    "Preco / Tamanho",
    "Preco", "Tamanho");
```

This new "PrecoM2" feature could provide valuable insights to the model by capturing an important relationship between size and price.

Additionally, ML.NET allows us to concatenate features easily:

```
var pipeline = contextoML.Transforms.Concatenate("Features", "Tamanho", "PrecoM2");
```

This operation combines our features into a single vector, which is the format that many ML algorithms expect.

Setting the Stage for Learning

These steps—loading, visualization, cleaning, transformation, and feature engineering—are essential to preparing your data for machine learning. They transform raw data into a refined, informative format that is ready to be consumed by learning algorithms.

In ML.NET, all these steps can be chained together into a single pipeline:

```
// Especificar pipeline de preparação de dados e treinamento do modelo, primeiro troca os vazios ela média
var pipeline = contextoML.Transforms.ReplaceMissingValues(
    outputColumnName: "TamanhoProcessado",
    inputColumnName: "Tamanho",
    replacementMode: MissingValueReplacingEstimator.ReplacementMode.Mean)
.Append(contextoML.Transforms.Concatenate("Features", new[] { "TamanhoProcessado" }))
.Append(contextoML.Regression.Trainers.Sdca(labelColumnName: "Preco", maximumNumberOfIterations: 100));
```

This pipeline encapsulates the entire data preparation and model training process into a single, cohesive structure. It's like creating a custom assembly line for your data, where each step refines and prepares it for the creation of the final model.

Remember, the quality of your model is highly dependent on the quality of the data you provide. Investing time in these preparation steps can make a significant difference in the final performance of your machine learning model.

Chapter 3: Regression in C# with ML.NET

Welcome, data explorers! Today we're going to dive into the fascinating world of linear and logistic regressions. Imagine you're a data detective, and these techniques are your magic magnifying glasses for uncovering patterns and making predictions. Let's break down these concepts in a way that's easy for you to understand!

Linear Regression: The Straight Line That Connects the Dots

What is Linear Regression?

Linear regression is like plotting the best straight line through a bunch of points on a graph. Imagine you're trying to predict the price of houses based on their size. Each house you know about is a point on the graph, with size on the X-axis and price on the Y-axis.

This was done in the example above on this command line (removing the other steps to make it clear which command was used)

```
var pipeline = contextoML.Transforms.Concatenate("Features", new[] { "Tamanho" })
    .Append(contextoML.Regression.Trainers.Sdca(labelColumnName: "Preco", maximumNumberOfIterations: 100));
```

This snippet of code is like telling our data detective, "Hey, use the size of the house to guess the price!"

How does it work?

- Data Collection: You gather information about several houses (size and price).
- Plot: Put this data on a graph.
- Drawing the Line: The algorithm tries to find the best straight line that passes as close as possible to all points.
- Equation of the Line: This line is described by a simple equation: $y = mx + b$
  - y is the price we want to predict
  - x is the size of the house
  - m is the slope of the line (how much the price changes for each additional square meter)
  - b is where the line crosses the Y-axis (the base price of a hypothetical zero-size house)

When to use?

Use linear regression when you want to predict a continuous number (such as price, temperature, height) based on one or more features.

Linear Regression Example – House Price Prediction

Class for Property Data and Prediction Response and then the code, which is available at https://github.com/wagnersalvi/LivroMaquinas

```csharp
using Microsoft.ML.Data;

namespace RegressaoLinear;

8 referências
public class DadosImovel
{
    [LoadColumn(0)]
    6 referências
    public float Tamanho { get; set; }

    [LoadColumn(1)]
    0 referências
    public float Quartos { get; set; }

    [LoadColumn(2)]
    4 referências
    public float Preco { get; set; }
}

1 referência
public class PredicaoImovel
{
    [ColumnName("Score")]
    1 referência
    public float PrecoPrevisao { get; set; }
}
```

```csharp
using Microsoft.ML;
using RegressaoLinear;

MLContext contextoML = new MLContext();

// Importar ou criar dados de treinamento
DadosImovel[] dadosCasas = new DadosImovel[]
{
    new DadosImovel { Tamanho = 50.0F, Preco = 150.0F },
    new DadosImovel { Tamanho = 75.0F, Preco = 225.0F },
    new DadosImovel { Tamanho = 100.0F, Preco = 300.0F },
    new DadosImovel { Tamanho = 125.0F, Preco = 375.0F },
    new DadosImovel { Tamanho = 150.0F, Preco = 450.0F },
    new DadosImovel { Tamanho = 175.0F, Preco = 525.0F },
    new DadosImovel { Tamanho = 200.0F, Preco = 600.0F }
};
IDataView dadosTreinamento = contextoML.Data.LoadFromEnumerable(dadosCasas);

// Especificar pipeline de preparação de dados e treinamento do modelo
var pipeline = contextoML.Transforms.Concatenate("Features", new[] { "Tamanho" })
               .Append(contextoML.Regression.Trainers.LbfgsPoissonRegression(labelColumnName: "Preco"));

// Treinar modelo
var modelo = pipeline.Fit(dadosTreinamento);

// Fazer uma previsão
var motorPrevisao = contextoML.Model.CreatePredictionEngine<DadosImovel, PredicaoImovel>(modelo);

for (int i = 50; i <= 250; i += 25)
{
    var dadoTeste = new DadosImovel { Tamanho = i };
    var previsao = motorPrevisao.Predict(dadoTeste);
    Console.WriteLine($"Tamanho: {i} m², Preço previsto: R${previsao.PrecoPrevisao:F2}");
}
```

The result is approximate to the one below:

Console de Depuração do Microsoft Visual Studio

```
Tamanho: 50 m², Preço previsto: R$185,22
Tamanho: 75 m², Preço previsto: R$227,83
Tamanho: 100 m², Preço previsto: R$280,24
Tamanho: 125 m², Preço previsto: R$344,70
Tamanho: 150 m², Preço previsto: R$423,99
Tamanho: 175 m², Preço previsto: R$521,53
Tamanho: 200 m², Preço previsto: R$641,49
Tamanho: 225 m², Preço previsto: R$789,06
Tamanho: 250 m², Preço previsto: R$970,56
```

Code Explanation

Initial Configuration

- Machine Learning Context: An instance of MLContext is created, which serves as the central point for all machine learning operations in this project.

Training Data Definition

- An array of PropertyData objects is created, with each object specifying a property size and its corresponding price.
- This data is then loaded into an IDataView, which is the format used by ML.NET to manipulate the data throughout the learning process.

Training Pipeline Configuration

- Feature Concatenation: Data points (only the size) are concatenated into a "Features" column. This is a common practice in ML.NET to define what data will be used as input to the model.
- Algorithm Selection: The LbfgsPoissonRegression algorithm is chosen to train the model. This algorithm is well suited for regression problems and is used here to model the relationship between property size and price.

Model Training

- Model Fit: With the pipeline configured, the model is trained using the already loaded training data.

Prediction

- A PredictionEngine is created to generate predictions with the trained model.
- Using a for loop, the code makes predictions for property sizes ranging from $50m^2$ to $250m^2$ in $25m^2$ increments.
- Each prediction generates a price estimate, which is then printed to the console.

Variation in results between runs of a linear regression model is a common phenomenon in machine learning and is related to several factors. Here is a conceptual explanation of the main reasons:

- Random parameter initialization: Many machine learning algorithms, including some used for linear regression, start with random values for model parameters (such as weights and biases). This random initialization can lead to different starting points in the parameter space, resulting in different final solutions.
- Stochastic nature of optimization algorithms: Algorithms such as Stochastic Gradient Descent (SGD), often used to optimize machine learning models, have a random component in the selection of samples for parameter updates. This can lead to different convergence paths and, consequently, different final results.
- Order of training data: If the algorithm processes the data in batches and the order of these batches is random, this can influence the learning path of the model and result in slight differences in the final model.
- Convergence to local minima: In non-convex optimization problems, the algorithm may converge to different local minima depending on the starting point and the path taken during optimization.
- Random data splitting: If you are randomly splitting your data into training and testing sets each run, this can result in different subsets of data being used to train and evaluate the model, leading to variations in the results.
- Regularization and dropout: Techniques such as L1/L2 regularization and dropout, used to prevent overfitting, can introduce randomness into the training process.

- Floating-point operations and numeric precision: In some cases, minute differences caused by floating-point operations in different orders can accumulate and lead to slightly different results.
- Parallelism and multithreading: In implementations that use parallel computing, the exact order of operations may vary between executions, leading to small differences in results.

It is important to note that for a well-conditioned simple linear regression model, these variations should generally be small and should not significantly affect the overall performance of the model. If you are seeing large variations in results between runs, this may indicate instability in the model or data, and may require further investigation.

To ensure reproducibility, many machine learning libraries offer the option to set a "seed" for their random number generators. This allows you to obtain the same results across multiple runs, as long as all other factors remain constant.

Types of Linear Regression in the ML.Net Library

Within the scope of linear regression, ML.NET provides several useful approaches to solving prediction problems, each adapting to different data characteristics and modeling needs.

1. Classical Linear Regression

Classical linear regression establishes a linear relationship between independent (predictor) variables and the dependent (target) variable. This technique is useful when a simple linear relationship between the variables is assumed.

```
var mlContext = new MLContext();
var data = mlContext.Data.LoadFromTextFile<ModelInput>("data.csv", separatorChar: ',', hasHeader: true);

var pipeline = mlContext.Transforms.Concatenate("Features", new[] { "Feature1","Feature2" })
  .Append(mlContext.Regression.Trainers.Sdca(labelColumnName: "Label", maximumNumberOfIterations: 100));
```

2. Ridge Regression (Regularization)

This technique adds a penalty to the coefficients to reduce overfitting, especially useful when there are many correlated variables. This regularization is controlled by the alpha parameter.

```
var pipeline = mlContext.Transforms.Concatenate("Features", new[] { "Feature1", "Feature2" })
  .Append(mlContext.Regression.Trainers.LbfgsPoissonRegression(labelColumnName: "Label", L2Regularization: 0.1f));
```

3. Lasso Regression

Lasso regression is similar to Ridge regression but can reduce the coefficients of some variables to zero, effectively selecting a subset of predictor variables. This is ideal for feature selection.

```
var pipeline = mlContext.Transforms.Concatenate("Features", new[] { "Feature1", "Feature2" })
  .Append(mlContext.Regression.Trainers.Sdca(labelColumnName: "Label", L1Regularization: 0.1f));
```

4. Elastic Net

Elastic Net is realized by combining L1 and L2 Regularization in the same Sdca trainer.

```
var pipeline = mlContext.Transforms.Concatenate("Features", new[] { "Feature1", "Feature2" })
  .Append(mlContext.Regression.Trainers.Sdca(labelColumnName: "Label", L1Regularization: 0.1f, L2Regularization: 0.2f));
```

Logistic Regression: The Master of Binary Classification

What is Logistic Regression?

Despite its name, logistic regression is actually used for classification. It's like a judge deciding "yes" or "no," "cat" or "dog," "spam" or "not spam." Instead of predicting a number, it predicts the probability of something falling into a category.

How does it work?

- Data Collection: You gather information about several cases, each with characteristics and a known classification.
- Transformation: The algorithm uses a special function (called a sigmoid) to transform the data into probabilities between 0 and 1.
- Decision Line: Instead of a straight line, an S-shaped curve is created that better separates the two categories.
- Prediction: For new cases, the model calculates the probability and decides the category based on a threshold (usually 0.5).

```
var pipeline = contextoML.Transforms.Concatenate("Features", new[] { "Caracteristica1", "Caracteristica2" })
    .Append(contextoML.BinaryClassification.Trainers.SdcaLogisticRegression(labelColumnName: "Rotulo"));
```

When to use?

Use logistic regression when you want to classify something into two distinct categories, such as approving or denying a loan, diagnosing a disease as present or absent, or predicting whether or not a customer will buy a product.

Logistic Regression Example – Product Evaluation Analysis

Class for the Evaluation Phrases and the Prediction Response and then the code, which is available at https://github.com/wagnersalvi/LivroMaquinas

```csharp
using Microsoft.ML.Data;

namespace RegressaoLogistica;

8 referências
public class DadosSentimento
{
    [LoadColumn(0)]
    8 referências
    public string FraseSentimento { get; set; }

    [LoadColumn(1), ColumnName("Label")]
    4 referências
    public bool SentimentoBom { get; set; }
}

// Classe para representar a previsão
1 referência
public class PredicaoSentimento
{
    [ColumnName("PredictedLabel")]
    2 referências
    public bool Predicao { get; set; }

    2 referências
    public float Probabilidade { get; set; }

    0 referências
    public float Score { get; set; }
}
```

```csharp
0 referências
class Program
{
    0 referências
    static void Main(string[] args)
    {
        // Criar contexto ML
        MLContext mlContext = new MLContext(seed: 0);

        // Preparar dados
        var sentimentos = new List<DadosSentimento>
        {
            new DadosSentimento { FraseSentimento = "Eu adoro este produto!", SentimentoBom = true },
            new DadosSentimento { FraseSentimento = "Produto horrivel", SentimentoBom = false },
            new DadosSentimento { FraseSentimento = "Ótima surpresa", SentimentoBom = true },
            new DadosSentimento { FraseSentimento = "Nunca mais compro este produto", SentimentoBom = false }
        };
        IDataView dadosTreinamento = mlContext.Data.LoadFromEnumerable(sentimentos);

        // Definir pipeline de treinamento
        var pipeline = mlContext.Transforms.Text.FeaturizeText(outputColumnName: "Features", inputColumnName: "FraseSentimento")
            .Append(mlContext.BinaryClassification.Trainers.SdcaLogisticRegression(labelColumnName: "Label", featureColumnName: "Features"));

        // Treinar o modelo
        var model = pipeline.Fit(dadosTreinamento);

        // Criar motor de previsão
        var predictionEngine = mlContext.Model.CreatePredictionEngine<DadosSentimento, PredicaoSentimento>(model);

        // Fazer previsões
        var testSentiment = new DadosSentimento { FraseSentimento = "Eu estou feliz com esta compra" };
        var prediction = predictionEngine.Predict(testSentiment);

        Console.WriteLine($"Sentimento: {testSentiment.FraseSentimento}");
        Console.WriteLine($"Previsão: {(prediction.Predicao ? "Positivo" : "Negativo")}");
        Console.WriteLine($"Probabilidade: {prediction.Probabilidade:P2}");

        testSentiment = new DadosSentimento { FraseSentimento = "Produto lixo" };
        prediction = predictionEngine.Predict(testSentiment);

        Console.WriteLine($"Sentimento: {testSentiment.FraseSentimento}");
        Console.WriteLine($"Previsão: {(prediction.Predicao ? "Positivo" : "Negativo")}");
        Console.WriteLine($"Probabilidade: {prediction.Probabilidade:P2}");
    }
}
```

The result is approximate to the one below:

```
C:\  Selecionar Console de Depuração do Microsoft Visual Studio
Sentimento: Eu estou feliz com esta compra
Previsão: Positivo
Probabilidade: 0,00%
Sentimento: Produto lixo
Previsão: Negativo
Probabilidade: 0,00%
```

The probability is zero because there is very little training data, which affects the result, and any data analysis is more accurate when there is more information.

Code Explanation

Creating the ML Context

- The MLContext is initialized, which is the entry point for ML.NET, ensuring that all subsequent machine learning operations use the same configuration and, in this case, also using a seed to ensure reproducibility in random processes.

Data Preparation

- A list of SentimentData is created, containing opinion phrases (SentimentPhrase) and a boolean (GoodSentiment) indicating whether the sentiment is positive (true) or negative (false).
- This data is loaded into an IDataView, the internal format that ML.NET uses to store data.

Training Pipeline Definition

- Text Featurization: Sentences are transformed into numeric vectors that can be used by the algorithm, through a method called FeaturizeText. This processes the text and defines its features in the "Features" column.
- Binary Classification Trainer: The pipeline includes the use of SdcaLogisticRegression for model training. This algorithm is suitable for binary classification problems, such as identifying sentiment.

Model Training

- The pipeline is fitted (or trained) with the training data using the Fit method, creating a model ready to make predictions.

Creating the Prediction Engine

- CreatePredictionEngine is used to create an engine that can make predictions based on new sentiment data inputs.

Make Predictions

- Two example sentences are created for testing, and are passed to the prediction engine.
- For each sentence, the engine returns a prediction of whether the sentiment is positive or negative and the probability of that classification.
- The results are displayed in the console, showing the phrase, the prediction (such as "Positive" or "Negative"), and the associated probability.

Types of Logistic Regression in the ML.Net Library

ML.NET is a powerful machine learning library for .NET developers who want to integrate machine learning models into their applications. In the domain of logistic regression, ML.NET offers sophisticated methods for solving binary and multiclass classification problems, essential where the desired output is categorical.

1. Binary Logistic Regression

Binary logistic regression is used to classify data into one of two possible classes. It is widely used in scenarios where the response is binary, such as "yes" or "no", 0 or 1, true or false.

```
var pipeline = mlContext.Transforms.Concatenate("Features", new[] { "Feature1", "Feature2" })
    .Append(mlContext.BinaryClassification.Trainers.LbfgsLogisticRegression(labelColumnName: "Label"));
```

2. Multiclass Logistic Regression

This technique extends logistic regression to scenarios with more than two classes. It is particularly useful in applications such as image recognition systems, where an image may belong to more than two categories.

```
var pipeline = mlContext.Transforms.Concatenate("Features", new[] { "Feature1", "Feature2", "Feature3" })
    .Append(mlContext.MulticlassClassification.Trainers.LbfgsMaximumEntropy(labelColumnName: "Label"));
```

3. Advanced Logistic Regression with Probability Calibration

In addition to simply predicting the class, it is sometimes useful to predict the probability of each class. This can be done by calibrating the probabilities within the logistic regression model, significantly improving the interpretation of the results.

```
var pipeline = mlContext.Transforms.Concatenate("Features", new[] { "Feature1", "Feature2" })
    .Append(mlContext.BinaryClassification.Trainers.SdcaLogisticRegression(labelColumnName: "Label")
    .Append(mlContext.BinaryClassification.Trainers.PlattCalibrator()));
```

Differences between Linear and Logistic regression models

- Forecast Type:
    - Linear: Predicts a continuous number (e.g. house price).
    - Logistic: Predicts a category or probability (e.g. chance of approving a loan).
- Curve Shape:
    - Linear: Straight line.

- o Logistics: S-curve.
- Interpretation:
  - Linear: "For every unit of X, Y changes by m units."
  - Logistics: "For each unit of X, the chance of Y being 1 changes by a factor of...".

Both linear and logistic regression are powerful tools in your data magic kit. The key is knowing when to use each:

- o If you are predicting a number (like price, height, temperature), go with linear.
- o If you're deciding between two categories (yes/no, cat/dog), logistics is your friend.

Remember, just as a magician doesn't reveal his tricks, a good data scientist always checks the quality of his predictions before presenting them to the world!

Chapter 4: Classification in C# with ML.NET

What is Classification?

Classification involves teaching a model to categorize data based on patterns identified during training. The model is given a labeled dataset and learns to predict the correct class for new inputs.

Example:

- An email system that classifies messages as "Spam" or "Not Spam".

- A model that identifies whether an image contains a "Cat", "Dog" or "Other Animal".

Classification Utilities

The classification is widely used in several areas, such as:

- **Fraud Detection:** Banks use classification models to identify fraudulent transactions.

- **Medical Diagnosis:** ML models can predict diseases based on tests and symptoms.

- **Facial and Pattern Recognition:** Applied in security, facial unlocking and monitoring.

- **Sentiment Analysis:** Automatic assessment of sentiments in product reviews and social networks.

- **Churn Prediction:** Companies predict which customers are most likely to cancel a service.

Advantages of Classification

- **Automation** → Reduces the need for human intervention.
  Accuracy → Well-trained models can outperform manual analysis.
  Speed → Responds quickly to large volumes of data.
  Scalability → Can be applied to multiple domains and problems.

Classification with ML.Net

ML.NET is a powerful library for integrating machine learning into .NET applications. This chapter explores the types of classification supported by this library, specifically binary and multiclass classification, and demonstrates how to apply these concepts to real-world problems.

Binary Classification

Supported Algorithms

- SdcaLogisticRegression: Ideal for binary classification tasks.
- FastTree: A gradient boosting algorithm suitable for classification improvements.

Example: Credit Analysis with FasTree but the command for SdcaLogisticRegression is also commented out

Predict credit approval based on factors such as income and debt.

Data class first

```csharp
7 referências
public class DadosCredito
{
    6 referências
    public float Renda { get; set; }
    6 referências
    public float Dividas { get; set; }
    4 referências
    public bool Aprovado { get; set; }
}

1 referência
public class PredicaoCredito
{
    [ColumnName("PredictedLabel")]
    1 referência
    public bool PredictedLabel { get; set; }

    [ColumnName("Probability")]
    1 referência
    public float Probability { get; set; }

    [ColumnName("Score")]
    0 referências
    public float Score { get; set; }
}
```

Below is the analysis code

```
using ClassificacaoCredito;
using Microsoft.ML;

0 referências
class Program
{
    0 referências
    static void Main(string[] args)
    {
        var mlContext = new MLContext();

        // Dados fictícios de análise de crédito
        var trainData = new List<DadosCredito>
        {
            new DadosCredito { Renda = 50000, Dividas = 20000, Aprovado = true },
            new DadosCredito { Renda = 40000, Dividas = 30000, Aprovado = false },
            new DadosCredito { Renda = 75000, Dividas = 10000, Aprovado = true },
            new DadosCredito { Renda = 30000, Dividas = 40000, Aprovado = false }
        };

        var trainingData = mlContext.Data.LoadFromEnumerable(trainData);

        // Pipeline de FastTree
        var pipeline = mlContext.Transforms.Concatenate("Features", new[] { "Renda", "Dividas" })
            .Append(mlContext.BinaryClassification.Trainers.FastTree(labelColumnName: "Aprovado", featureColumnName: "Features"));

        //Pipeline de SdcaLogisticRegression
        //var pipeline = mlContext.Transforms.Concatenate("Features", new[] { "Renda", "Dividas" })
        //    .Append(mlContext.BinaryClassification.Trainers.SdcaLogisticRegression(labelColumnName: "Aprovado", featureColumnName: "Features"));

        // Treinando o modelo
        var model = pipeline.Fit(trainingData);

        // Fazendo previsões
        var predictionEngine = mlContext.Model.CreatePredictionEngine<DadosCredito, PredicanCredito>(model);

        var newCreditData = new DadosCredito { Renda = 60000, Dividas = 15000 };
        var prediction = predictionEngine.Predict(newCreditData);

        Console.WriteLine($"Renda: {newCreditData.Renda}, Divida: {newCreditData.Dividas}");
        Console.WriteLine($"Aprovação do Empréstimo? {(prediction.PredictedLabel ? "Sim" : "Não")}");
        Console.WriteLine($"Probabilidade: {prediction.Probability:P2}");
    }
}
```

The result will be something similar to the window below.

```
Console de Depuração do Microsoft Visual Studio
Renda: 60000, Dívida: 15000
Aprovação do Empréstimo? Não
Probabilidade: 50,00%
```

Code Explanation

Initial Configuration

- Creates a machine learning context (MLContext), which is required for any ML.NET project. It centralizes ML configuration and operations.

Training Data Definition

- Creates a list of CreditData that serves as a training database. Each item contains information on Income, Debts and whether the credit was Approved or not.
- This data is converted to an IDataView, the internal format used by ML.NET to manipulate the dataset.

Training Pipeline Configuration

- Feature Concatenation: The Income and Debt columns are combined into the "Features" column. This is a common preparation to indicate the attributes that will be considered by the model to make predictions.
- Classification Trainer Choice: Uses FastTree, a boosting algorithm that is robust to binary classification problems, to learn the relationship between income, debt, and credit approval.
- There is also commented code for using SdcaLogisticRegression, another popular algorithm for binary classification, showing flexibility in using different algorithms.

Model Training

- With the pipeline configured, Fit is used to fit the model to the training data. This process instructs the model to identify patterns in the data.

Making Predictions

- A PredictionEngine is created to perform fast and individual predictions.

- A new CreditData instance represents a new credit applicant. The model uses Income and Debt to predict whether the loan would be approved.
- The forecast results in:
  - PredictedLabel: Defines whether the credit is approved (true) or not (false).
  - Probability: Estimate of confidence in the forecast.

Forecast Output

- The forecast result is displayed in the console, showing income, debt, possibility of approval and the associated probability.

Multiclass Classification

Supported Algorithm

- SdcaMaximumEntropy: An efficient algorithm for multiclass classification.

Example: News Classification with SdcaMaximumEntropy

Sort news articles into categories like "Technology", "Sports", and "Politics".

Let's start with the data classes

```csharp
15 referências
public class Noticia
{
    12 referências
    public string TextoArtigo { get; set; }
    11 referências
    public string Categoria { get; set; }
}

1 referência
public class PredicaoNoticia
{
    [ColumnName("PredictedLabel")]
    2 referências
    public string Categoria { get; set; }

    4 referências
    public float[] Score { get; set; }
}
```

After that we will create the information for training and load the data into the model.

```csharp
var mlContext = new MLContext();

// Dados de treinamento
var noticias = new List<Noticia>
{
    new Noticia { TextoArtigo = "O uso de inteligência artificial...", Categoria = "Tecnologia" },
    new Noticia { TextoArtigo = "Computadores avançados para empresas", Categoria = "Tecnologia" },
    new Noticia { TextoArtigo = "Final do campeonato mundial de futebol", Categoria = "Esportes" },
    new Noticia { TextoArtigo = "Novos recordes na NBA", Categoria = "Esportes" },
    new Noticia { TextoArtigo = "Eleições presidenciais em debate", Categoria = "Política" },
    new Noticia { TextoArtigo = "Reforma tributária em discussão", Categoria = "Política" }
};

// Carregar os dados no ML.NET
var trainData = mlContext.Data.LoadFromEnumerable(noticias);
```

After that we create the model as below

```
// Pipeline de treinamento
var pipeline = mlContext.Transforms.Conversion.MapValueToKey("Label", nameof(Noticia.Categoria)) // Converte categoria para chave numérica
    .Append(mlContext.Transforms.Text.FeaturizeText("Features", nameof(Noticia.TextoArtigo))) // Vetorização do texto
    .Append(mlContext.MulticlassClassification.Trainers.SdcaMaximumEntropy("Label", "Features")) // Modelo de classificação
    .Append(mlContext.Transforms.Conversion.MapKeyToValue("PredictedLabel", "Label")); // Converte chave numérica de volta para string

// Treinar o modelo
var model = pipeline.Fit(trainData);

// Criar um motor de predição
var predictionEngine = mlContext.Model.CreatePredictionEngine<Noticia, PredicaoNoticia>(model);
```

And finally, we will create the test generation of any news item and print the category it fits into.

```
// Testar uma nova notícia
var newArticle = new Noticia { TextoArtigo = "Computador do presidente explodiu assistindo futebol" };
var prediction = predictionEngine.Predict(newArticle);

// Obter os nomes das categorias manualmente
var categorias = noticias.Select(n => n.Categoria).Distinct().OrderBy(c => c).ToList();

var predictions = model.Transform(trainData);

// Exibir a predição
Console.WriteLine($"Artigo: {newArticle.TextoArtigo}");

// Diagnóstico: verificar se há valores
if (!string.IsNullOrEmpty(prediction.Categoria))
{
    Console.WriteLine($"Categoria Predita: {prediction.Categoria}\n");
}
else
{
    int categoriaIndex = Array.IndexOf(prediction.Score, prediction.Score.Max());
    string categoriaPredita = categorias[categoriaIndex];

    Console.WriteLine($"\nCategoria Predita: {categoriaPredita}");
}
```

It is also possible to evaluate the percentage of each category for that text through the Score

```
// Exibir pontuação das categorias
Console.WriteLine("Pontuação das categorias:");
for (int i = 0; i < prediction.Score.Length; i++)
{
    string categoriaNome = (i < categorias.Count) ? categorias[i] : $"Categoria_{i}";
    Console.WriteLine($"{categoriaNome}: {prediction.Score[i]:F4}");
}
```

The result will be something similar to the window below.

```
Console de Depuração do Microsoft Visual Studio
Artigo: Computador do presidente explodiu assistindo futebol

Categoria Predita: Política
Pontuação das categorias:
Esportes: 0,1559
Política: 0,7523
Tecnologia: 0,0919
```

Model Evaluation

After developing models, it is crucial to evaluate them to ensure accuracy and reliability.

- Accuracy: Proportion of correct predictions.
- Precision: Proportion of true positives over all predicted positives.
- Recall: Proportion of true positives over all actual positives.

Evaluation Example using the news classification from the previous example

```csharp
// Criar conjunto de teste
var testNoticias = new List<Noticia>
{
    new Noticia { TextoArtigo = "Nova tecnologia de smartphones...", Categoria = "Tecnologia" },
    new Noticia { TextoArtigo = "Time de basquete vence o campeonato", Categoria = "Esportes" },
    new Noticia { TextoArtigo = "Eleições para governador acontecem neste domingo", Categoria = "Politica" }
};

var testData = mlContext.Data.LoadFromEnumerable(testNoticias);

// Fazer previsões no conjunto de teste
var transformedData = model.Transform(testData);

// Avaliação do modelo
var metrics = mlContext.MulticlassClassification.Evaluate(transformedData, labelColumnName: "Label", predictedLabelColumnName: "PredictedLabel");

// Exibir métricas do modelo
Console.WriteLine($"\nMétricas do Modelo:");
Console.WriteLine($"Acurácia Macro: {metrics.MacroAccuracy:P2}");
Console.WriteLine($"Acurácia Micro: {metrics.MicroAccuracy:P2}");
Console.WriteLine($"Log-Loss: {metrics.LogLoss:F4}");
Console.WriteLine($"Log-Loss por Classe: {string.Join(", ", metrics.PerClassLogLoss.Select(l => l.ToString("F4")))}");

Console.WriteLine("\nAvaliação concluída!");
```

Which will result in

```
Avaliando o modelo...

Métricas do Modelo:
Acurácia Macro: 66,67%
Acurácia Micro: 66,67%
Log-Loss: 0,5959
Log-Loss por Classe: 0,6077, 0,3812, 0,7989

Avaliação concluída!
```

Results of model evaluations

1. Macro Accuracy

Macro Accuracy is the average of the individual accuracies of each class. In other words, it measures performance equally for all classes, regardless of the number of examples in each category.

How is it calculated?

For each class Ci , we calculate the hit rate (number of correct predictions for that class divided by the total number of examples for that class). Then, we average it across all classes.

Formula:

Macro Accuracy $=$

$$\frac{1}{N} \sum_{i=1}^{N} \frac{Amostras\ corretamente\ classificadas\ da\ classe\ i}{Total\ de\ Amostras\ da\ classe\ i}$$

Where N is the total number of classes

Example:

Suppose we have a test set with **3 classes** :

- **Technology** : 90% accuracy

- **Sports** : 70% correct

- **Politics** : 80% correct

Macro accuracy would be:

$$\frac{90\% + 70\% + 80\%}{3} = 80\%$$

It is used when classes have different amounts of examples and we want to measure the model performance in a balanced way for all categories.

2. Micro Accuracy

Micro Accuracy measures the overall performance of the model considering the total number of correct and incorrect predictions, without separating by class.

How is it calculated?

It is the total proportion of correct predictions over the total number of examples, without dividing by class.

Formula:

$$Micro\ Accuracy = \frac{Total\ de\ previsões\ corretas}{Total\ de\ exemplos\ no\ conjunto\ de\ teste}$$

Example:

If we have:

- 100 examples in total
- 85 were classified correctly
  So:

$$MicroAccuracy = \frac{85}{100} = 85\%$$

It is used when all classes have similar amounts of examples, as it favors the most common categories and when we want to measure the overall performance of the model.

3. Log-Loss (Logarithmic Loss)

Log-Loss measures how confident the model's predictions are. Unlike accuracy, which only tells whether the prediction was correct or incorrect, Log-Loss penalizes incorrect predictions made with high confidence.

How is it calculated?

Each model prediction generates probabilities for each class. Log-Loss compares the predicted probability for the correct class with the expected probability (1 for the correct class, 0 for all others).

Formula

$$LogLoss = -\frac{1}{N}\sum_{i=1}^{N}\sum_{j=1}^{C} y_{i,j}\, log(p_{i,j})$$

Where:

- N is the total number of samples
- C is the total number of classes
- $y_{i,j}$ is 1 if sample i belongs to class j and 0 otherwise
- $p_{i,j}$ is the probability predicted by the model for class j

Example:

Suppose we have a sporting item, and the model gives the following probabilities:

- **Sports:** 70% (correct)

- **Politics:** 20%

- **Technology:** 10%

Log-Loss takes the logarithm of the probability of the correct class (70%):

$$LogLoss = -\log(0.7) = 0.154$$

If the model was wrong and predicted Policy with 90%, the Log-Loss would be:

$$LogLoss = -\log(0.1) = 1.0$$

The lower the Log-Loss, the better! A value close to 0 indicates confident and correct predictions, while a high value indicates that the model is confidently missing the mark.

When to use?

- When we want to measure not only the accuracy of the model, but also its confidence in the predictions.

4. Log-Loss by Class

Log-Loss per class is the same calculation as Log-Loss, but done separately for each category. This allows you to see in which categories the model has more uncertainty.

Example output:

Log-Loss by Class: 0.3154, 0.2876, 0.2829

- **0.3154** → The model has more uncertainty in this class.

- **0.2829** → The model has less uncertainty in this class.

If a category has a very high Log-Loss, it may be a sign that there are too few examples of that category in the training.

Summary of Evaluation Metrics

Metric	Meaning	Interval	Best value
Macro Accuracy	Average class accuracy	0% to 100%	The bigger the better
Micro Accuracy	Total hit ratio	0% to 100%	The bigger the better

Log-Loss	Measures the confidence of the model	0 to ∞	The smaller the better
Log-Loss by class	Specific Log-Loss for each category	0 to ∞	The smaller the better

When to use which metric?

- If classes have uneven distributions → Use Macro Accuracy

- If there are balanced classes → Use Micro Accuracy

- If we want to measure the confidence of the model → Use Log-Loss

- If we want to know in which classes the model has more uncertainty → Use Log-Loss per class

Chapter 5: Clustering in C# with ML.NET

What is Clustering?

Clustering is an unsupervised machine learning technique used to group similar data into subsets called clusters. Unlike classification, where data has predefined labels, in clustering the goal is to identify hidden patterns without prior knowledge of the categories.

How does clustering work?

Clustering algorithms analyze the characteristics of the data and group elements that have similarities between them, minimizing differences within the group and maximizing differences between different groups.

Clusters can be defined based on:

- **Distance between points** (example: Euclidean metric)
- **Data density** (example: DBSCAN)
- **Statistical distribution** (example: Gaussian Mixture Models)

Main Clustering Algorithms

1. K-Means

Divides the data into **K groups** by choosing initial centroids and adjusting the groups iteratively.

- **Advantage** : Simple and efficient for large volumes of data.

- **Disadvantage** : It is necessary to define the K value in advance.

2. DBSCAN (Density-Based Spatial Clustering of Applications with Noise)

Groups data based on **density** , making it ideal for irregularly shaped data.

- **Advantage** : Identifies outliers as noise.
- **Disadvantage** : Sensitive to the choice of parameters.

3. Hierarchical Clustering

Creates a hierarchy of clusters that can be represented by a **dendrogram** .

- **Advantage** : No need to define the number of clusters in advance.
- **Disadvantage** : Can be computationally expensive for large datasets.

Practical Example of Clustering

Suppose a company has customer data and wants to segment them based on purchasing patterns. Using the K-Means algorithm, we can group customers into clusters, such as:

- **Group 1:** Customers who make frequent small-value purchases.

- **Group 2:** Customers who make few but high-value purchases.
- **Group 3:** Customers who only buy seasonally.

With this information, the company can customize marketing strategies for each group, increasing the effectiveness of campaigns.

Advantages of Clustering

- **Identifies hidden patterns** without the need for labels.
- **Reduces data complexity** , making analysis easier.
- **Applicable to various sectors** , such as marketing, biology, security and more.

Using the ML.NET Library for Clustering

The library supports K-Means. The library does not have out-of-the-box support for more complex methods like DBSCAN or hierarchical clustering. This does not mean that you cannot use or experiment with other techniques in a .NET context, but rather that you can integrate or complement ML.NET with other libraries or frameworks.

C# Clustering Example

Model Class

```csharp
using Microsoft.ML.Data;

namespace Clustering;

0 referências
class Cliente
{
    [LoadColumn(0)] public float GastoMensal;
    [LoadColumn(1)] public float FrequenciaCompras;
}

0 referências
class ClusterPrediction
{
    [ColumnName("PredictedLabel")] public uint Cluster;
}
```

C# Code

```csharp
using Clustering;
using Microsoft.ML;

0 referências
class Program
{
    0 referências
    static void Main()
    {
        var context = new MLContext();
        var dados = new[]
        {
            new Cliente { GastoMensal = 200, FrequenciaCompras = 5 },
            new Cliente { GastoMensal = 50, FrequenciaCompras = 2 },
            new Cliente { GastoMensal = 1000, FrequenciaCompras = 10 },
            new Cliente { GastoMensal = 150, FrequenciaCompras = 3 }
        };

        var dataView = context.Data.LoadFromEnumerable(dados);
        var pipeline = context.Transforms.Concatenate("Features", "GastoMensal", "FrequenciaCompras")
                    .Append(context.Clustering.Trainers.KMeans("Features", numberOfClusters: 3));

        var modelo = pipeline.Fit(dataView);
        var predictor = context.Model.CreatePredictionEngine<Cliente, ClusterPrediction>(modelo);

        var novoCliente = new Cliente { GastoMensal = 120, FrequenciaCompras = 4 };
        var resultado = predictor.Predict(novoCliente);

        Console.WriteLine($"O cliente foi classificado no cluster: {resultado.Cluster}");
    }
}
```

The result of Clustering is:

```
Console de Depuração do Microsoft Visual Studio

O cliente foi classificado no cluster: 2
```

Code Explanation

ML Context Configuration

- MLContext: Initializes the machine learning context that sets up the environment for ML.NET operations such as loading data, configuring pipelines, and training models.

Data Preparation

- An array of Customer objects is created. Each Customer has attributes such as MonthlyExpense and PurchaseFrequency.
- This data is loaded into an IDataView, which is ML.NET's standard format for processing collections of data.

Training Pipeline Definition

- Concatenation of Features: The MonthlyExpense and PurchaseFrequency properties are combined into a single "Features" column. This column represents the input data for the clustering algorithm.
- K-Means Clustering Trainer: Configure the K-Means trainer to group data into 3 clusters. K-Means is an unsupervised learning algorithm used to divide data instances into k groups based on their input variables.

Model Training

- Fit: With the pipeline configured, the Fit method adjusts the model to our data, creating groups based on the similarities of the provided features.

- A PredictionEngine is created to associate new data with an existing cluster.
- A new customer is defined with MonthlyExpense and PurchaseFrequency values. Based on this data, PredictionEngine classifies the customer into one of the clusters previously determined by the model.

Exit

- The prediction result is printed to the console, showing which cluster the new Client was assigned to.

Chapter 6: Time Series Analysis in C#

Concept of Time Series

Imagine you're watching waves come and go on a beach. Each wave has a pattern: it rises, peaks, and then recedes. This repetitive, temporal movement is the essence of what we call time series. They're simply sequences of data over time, and analyzing them is a powerful tool in the world of machine learning.

Time series are collections of data points indexed chronologically. Unlike regular data that can be shuffled, time series are dependent on the order of events. Consider stock prices, weather data, heart rate, and even the daily number of active users on an online platform. All of these situations are time-dependent, which requires special approaches to analysis and forecasting.

Why Time Series?

Time series analysis allows us to predict future values based on past patterns, detecting trends and seasonality. It is like reading a diary that reveals the 'mood' of a system over time. In recent years, the use of machine learning methods for time series has become crucial in several areas, from financial forecasting to predictive maintenance of industrial machines.

Practical Applications

Demand and Inventory Prediction: Large retail chains use time series to predict demand for different products at different times of the year. This helps optimize inventory, avoiding shortages and excesses.

- **Financial Analysis:** In the financial market, time series forecasting is used to predict the prices of stocks and other assets. Complex algorithms analyze a large amount of historical data to suggest the best time to buy or sell.
- **Health Monitoring:** In wearable health devices like smartwatches, time series help monitor and predict anomalies in users' vital signs, such as heart rate or sleep patterns, alerting them to potential problems before they happen.
- **Industrial Quality Control:** Manufacturing companies use time series models to predict when a machine might fail,

allowing maintenance to be performed before a breakdown occurs, increasing the efficiency of operations.

Machine Learning Techniques for Time Series

- **Classical Models:** Techniques such as ARIMA (AutoRegressive Integrated Moving Average) and SARIMA are popular for capturing cyclical patterns and trends in stationary time series.
- **Recurrent Neural Networks (RNNs):** These are specially designed for sequential data and are valued for their ability to handle long-term dependencies.
- **Prophet:** Developed by Facebook, it is a powerful tool for modeling time series, especially when there are pronounced seasonal components. It is particularly easy to use, even for beginners.
- **Models Based on Random Forests and Gradient Boosting:** Tools such as Random Forest and Boosted Trees can be adapted for time series, with modifications to deal with the temporal structure of the data.

C# Time Series Example

For time series forecasting, you need to install the package below

```
dotnet add package Microsoft.ML.TimeSeries
```

Model:

```csharp
// Classe representando os dados de entrada
using Microsoft.ML.Data;

10 referências
public class Venda
{
    [LoadColumn(0)]
    8 referências
    public float Semana { get; set; }

    [LoadColumn(1)]
    9 referências
    public float Quantidade { get; set; }
}


// Classe para armazenar os resultados da previsão
2 referências
public class PrevisaoVendas
{
    [ColumnName("QuantidadePrevista")]
    3 referências
    public float[] QuantidadePrevista { get; set; }
}
```

Code Analysis:

```csharp
0 referências
static void Main()
{
    // Inicializa o contexto ML.NET
    var mlContext = new MLContext();

    // Dados históricos de vendas (exemplo: vendas semanais)
    var dadosVendas = new[]
    {
        new Venda() { Semana = 1, Quantidade = 200 },
        new Venda() { Semana = 2, Quantidade = 250 },
        new Venda() { Semana = 3, Quantidade = 270 },
        new Venda() { Semana = 4, Quantidade = 300 },
        new Venda() { Semana = 5, Quantidade = 320 },
        new Venda() { Semana = 6, Quantidade = 340 },
        new Venda() { Semana = 7, Quantidade = 390 },
        new Venda() { Semana = 8, Quantidade = 410 }
    };

    // Converte os dados para IDataView
    var dataView = mlContext.Data.LoadFromEnumerable(dadosVendas);

    // Configura a pipeline para previsão de séries temporais
    var pipeline = mlContext.Forecasting.ForecastBySsa(
        outputColumnName: nameof(PrevisaoVendas.QuantidadePrevista),
        inputColumnName: nameof(Venda.Quantidade),
        windowSize: 3,        // Número de pontos usados para análise
        seriesLength: 8,      // Tamanho da série completa
        trainSize: 8,         // Quantidade de dados usados para treinar
        horizon: 3);          // Número de previsões futuras

    // Treina o modelo
    var model = pipeline.Fit(dataView);

    // Criando um mecanismo de previsão
    var forecastingEngine = model.CreateTimeSeriesEngine<Venda, PrevisaoVendas>(mlContext);

    // Fazendo previsões para as próximas 3 semanas
    var previsao = forecastingEngine.Predict();

    // Exibe os resultados
    Console.WriteLine("Previsão de vendas para as próximas semanas:");
    for (int i = 0; i < previsao.QuantidadePrevista.Length; i++)
    {
        Console.WriteLine($"Semana {dadosVendas.Length + i + 1}: {previsao.QuantidadePrevista[i]:0}");
    }
}
```

Execution result

🖾 Console de Depuração do Microsoft Visual Studio

```
Previsão de vendas para as próximas semanas:
Semana 9: 453
Semana 10: 493
Semana 11: 537
```

Code Explanation

ML.NET Context Configuration

- Initializes a machine learning context (MLContext), required for any operation in ML.NET, managing the entire ML process.

Sales Data Definition

- Creates a list of Sale objects, where each instance represents sales in a specific week (Week) with the corresponding quantity (Quantity).
- This data represents historical weekly sales data.

Conversion to IDataView

- Converts the sales data list (array) into an IDataView, which is ML.NET's data manipulation format, preparing this data for training.

Setting Up the Time Series Forecasting Pipeline

- ForecastBySsa: Configures the pipeline with the ForecastBySsa transformation, which performs time series forecasting.
- outputColumnName: Names the output column for predictions.
- inputColumnName: Indicates which input column (sales quantity) is analyzed.
- windowSize: Specifies the number of data points used to analyze the pattern of the series (in this case, 3 weeks).
- seriesLength: Sets the length of the total series for analysis.

- trainSize: Amount of historical data used for training.
- horizon: Number of future periods for which the forecast will be made (3 weeks).

Model Training
- The model is trained using the Fit method, using historical data to understand sales patterns.

Creation of the Forecasting Mechanism
- A TimeSeriesEngine is created to perform time series predictions using the trained model.
- This engine uses the trained transformation to generate predictions for future points in the time series.

Forecasting and Displaying Results
- The forecasting engine (forecastingEngine) is used to forecast sales for the next 3 weeks.
- Forecast results are displayed, indicating predicted weekly sales amounts for upcoming periods based on historical data.

Chapter 7 : Natural Language Processing (NLP)

NLP Fundamentals

Natural Language Processing (NLP) is one of the most fascinating areas of artificial intelligence. It allows machines to understand, interpret and generate human language in increasingly sophisticated ways. If you've ever spoken to a chatbot, dictated text on your phone or seen an automatic translator in action, you've already used NLP without realizing it!

NLP is the bridge between human language and computing. It combines techniques from linguistics, statistics, and machine learning to enable computers to understand and manipulate text and speech. Its goal is to reduce the barrier between the natural communication of humans and the formal logic of machines.

NLP Applications

NLP applications are everywhere, impacting different sectors:

- **Chatbots and Virtual Assistants** : Alexa, Google Assistant, and Siri are practical examples of NLP in action.

- **Machine Translation** : Services like Google Translate have evolved thanks to advanced NLP models.

- **Sentiment Analysis** : Companies use NLP to understand what customers think about their products from reviews and social media.

- **Spell Check and Autocomplete** : Tools like Grammarly and your phone's own spell checker use NLP to improve your writing.

- **Intelligent Search** : Search engines like Google interpret complex queries and suggest relevant results using NLP.

NLP Features

For NLP to work, it needs to address complex challenges such as:

- **Ambiguity** : Words can have different meanings depending on the context.

- **Synonyms and Variations** : Different expressions can have the same meaning.

- **Grammatical Errors** : Humans write and speak informally and often incorrectly.

- **Slang and Dialects** : The meaning of words can vary depending on culture and location.

Popular NLP Models

Advances in NLP have been driven by powerful machine learning models such as:

- **Bag of Words (BoW) and TF-IDF:** Simpler models that represent texts as numeric vectors based on word frequency.
- **Word Embeddings (Word2Vec, GloVe, FastText):** Techniques that transform words into richer vector

representations, allowing models to understand semantic relationships between words.

- **Recurrent Neural Networks (RNN) and LSTMs:** Models capable of handling sequences of words and understanding the previous context in a text.
- **Transformers (BERT, GPT, T5):** Today's most advanced models, such as ChatGPT, are based on this architecture, enabling deep understanding of language and generation of highly coherent texts.

Example of evaluating sentiment on product opinions

Model Class:

```
using Microsoft.ML.Data;

namespace ExemploNLP;

14 referências
public class TreinamentoSentimento
{
    12 referências
    public string Opiniao { get; set; }
    11 referências
    public string Avaliacao { get; set; }
}

1 referência
public class PredicaoSentimento
{
    [ColumnName("PredictedLabel")]
    2 referências
    public string Avaliacao { get; set; }

    4 referências
    public float[] Score { get; set; }
}
```

C# code for creating the model

```csharp
var mlContext = new MLContext();

// Dados de treinamento
var treinamento = new List<TreinamentoSentimento>
{
    new TreinamentoSentimento { Opiniao = "Adorei o produto, atendendo minhas expectativas", Avaliacao = "Boa" },
    new TreinamentoSentimento { Opiniao = "Funcionamento perfeito", Avaliacao = "Boa" },
    new TreinamentoSentimento { Opiniao = "Aprovado e muito útil", Avaliacao = "Boa" },
    new TreinamentoSentimento { Opiniao = "Recomendo o produto", Avaliacao = "Boa" },
    new TreinamentoSentimento { Opiniao = "Bom investimento", Avaliacao = "Boa" },

    new TreinamentoSentimento { Opiniao = "Não vale o investimento", Avaliacao = "Ruim" },
    new TreinamentoSentimento { Opiniao = "Não funciona", Avaliacao = "Ruim" },
    new TreinamentoSentimento { Opiniao = "Produto parou de funcionar", Avaliacao = "Ruim" },
    new TreinamentoSentimento { Opiniao = "Devolvi por que não me atendeu", Avaliacao = "Ruim" },
};

// Carregar os dados no ML.NET
var trainData = mlContext.Data.LoadFromEnumerable(treinamento);

// Pipeline de treinamento
var pipeline = mlContext.Transforms.Conversion.MapValueToKey("Label", nameof(TreinamentoSentimento.Avaliacao)) // Converte avaliacao para chave
    .Append(mlContext.Transforms.Text.FeaturizeText("Features", nameof(TreinamentoSentimento.Opiniao))) // Vetorização do texto
    .Append(mlContext.MulticlassClassification.Trainers.SdcaMaximumEntropy("Label", "Features")) // Modelo de classificação
    .Append(mlContext.Transforms.Conversion.MapKeyToValue("PredictedLabel", "Label")); // Converte chave numérica de volta para string

// Treinar o modelo
var model = pipeline.Fit(trainData);

// Criar um motor de predição
var predictionEngine = mlContext.Model.CreatePredictionEngine<TreinamentoSentimento, PredicaoSentimento>(model);
```

C# code for model testing

```csharp
// Testar uma uma nova opinião
var novaopiniao = new TreinamentoSentimento { Opiniao = "Atendeu minhas expectativas" };
var prediction = predictionEngine.Predict(novaopiniao);

// Obter os nomes das avaliacao manualmente
var avaliacao = treinemento.Select(n => n.Avaliacao).Distinct().OrderBy(c => c).ToList();

var predictions = model.Transform(trainData);

// Exibir a predição
Console.WriteLine($"Opinião: {novaopiniao.Opiniao}");

// Diagnóstico: verificar se há valores
if (!string.IsNullOrEmpty(prediction.Avaliacao))
{
    Console.WriteLine($"Avaliacao Predita: {prediction.Avaliacao}\n");
}
else
{
    int avaliacaoIndex = Array.IndexOf(prediction.Score, prediction.Score.Max());
    string avaliacaoPredita = avaliacao[avaliacaoIndex];

    Console.WriteLine($"\nAvaliação Predita: {avaliacaoPredita}");

}

// Exibir pontuação das categorias
Console.WriteLine("Pontuação das Avaliações:");
for (int i = 0; i < prediction.Score.Length; i++)
{
    string avaliacaoNome = (i < avaliacao.Count) ? avaliacao[i] : $"Avaliacao_{i}";
    Console.WriteLine($"{avaliacaoNome}: {prediction.Score[i]:F4}");
}
```

Evaluation result:

```
C:\ Console de Depuração do Microsoft Visual Studio
Opinião: Atendeu minhas expectativas

Avaliação Predita: Boa
Pontuação das Avaliações:
Boa: 0,9586
Ruim: 0,0414
```

In this case above, he mentions that there is a 95% chance of being a good evaluation and, like any model, the more training data we have, where it is manually evaluated and passed through the training process, the greater the effectiveness of the results. With little data, it will be less accurate and there will be a greater chance of errors.

Code Explanation

Creating the ML.NET Context

- An MLContext is initialized to define the machine learning environment, serving as the central point for ML.NET operations.

Training Data Definition

- Creates a list of TrainingSentiment, where each instance contains an Opinion (the text) and an associated Rating (which can be "Good" or "Bad").
- Loads this data into an IDataView, the internal representation of data in ML.NET.

Training Pipeline Configuration

- Key Value Conversion: Ratings ("Good" or "Bad") are converted to numeric values (keys) using MapValueToKey, allowing them to be processed during training.
- Text Featurization: FeaturizeText converts words into numeric vectors, essential for the model to be able to interpret and use the text as input.
- Multiclass Classifier: Uses SdcaMaximumEntropy, a multiclass classification algorithm, to train the model based on the vectorized features.
- Converting Predictions Back: MapKeyToValue transforms numeric predictions back to their original categories ("Good" or "Bad") after classification.

Model Training

- Fit: The pipeline is fitted to the training data, creating a model that can predict future sentiment-based ratings.

Creating the Prediction Engine

- A PredictionEngine is instantiated to predict ratings of new opinions.

Test the Model

- A new TrainingSentiment is created with an opinion ("Met my expectations") for verification.
- Predict determines the predicted rating for this new opinion.

Displaying Results

- Shows the original opinion and the predicted rating. If there is no prediction, uses the maximum score to infer the rating.
- Displays the score for each assessment category, showing the probability calculated by the model for each.

Chapter 8 : Neural Networks and Deep Learning in C#

Basic concepts of neural networks and Deep Learning

Imagine a world where machines can see, hear, speak, and even create art. A world where algorithms can diagnose diseases with greater accuracy than experienced doctors, or predict market trends with incredible accuracy. This world is not science fiction - it is the reality we are living in, thanks to neural networks and deep learning.

Artificial neural networks are like the nervous system of the digital world. Just as our brain is made up of billions of interconnected neurons, a neural network is made up of layers of artificial "neurons" that process and transmit information[1]. Each neuron receives inputs, performs calculations and produces an output, creating a flow of information that allows the network to "learn" and make decisions.

Think of each neuron as a little detective, analyzing clues and passing on its findings. The more layers of detectives we have, the more complex mysteries we can solve—and that's where deep learning comes in.

Deep Learning: Diving into the Depths of Data

Deep learning is like diving into an ocean of data in a high-tech submarine. While simple neural networks stay on the surface, deep learning networks dive deep, exploring layers and layers of information.

These deep networks are capable of identifying extremely complex patterns. It's as if each layer of the network learns to recognize increasingly abstract features. For example, when analyzing an image, the first layers can detect edges and simple shapes, while the deeper layers can recognize entire objects or even entire contexts.

Types of Neural Networks: A Zoo of Artificial Intelligence

Just as there are different species of animals adapted to different environments, we also have different types of neural networks specialized in different tasks:

- **Convolutional Neural Networks (CNNs):** These are the "eyes" of the digital world. Specialized in image processing, these networks are responsible for facial recognition, object detection and even medical imaging diagnosis.
- **Recurrent Neural Networks (RNNs):** Think of them as the "ear" and "voice" of AI. They're perfect for handling sequences, like text and audio. They're the powerhouse behind virtual assistants, machine translation, and even music composition.

- **Generative Adversarial Networks (GANs):** These are the "artists" of the AI world. These networks consist of two competing models: one to create convincing fake data, and the other to detect fakes. The result? GANs can generate incredibly realistic images, music, and even text.

Applications: From Fiction to Reality

The impact of neural networks and deep learning on our lives is as profound as it is fascinating. Let's look at some examples:

- **Healthcare:** Neural networks are revolutionizing medical diagnosis, detecting tumors in X-ray images with accuracy comparable to or greater than that of experienced radiologists.
- **Finance:** Deep learning algorithms analyze complex patterns in market data to predict trends and detect fraud in real time.
- **Transportation:** Autonomous vehicles use neural networks to "see" their surroundings, make decisions, and navigate safely.

- **Entertainment:** Streaming platforms like Netflix and Spotify use deep learning to recommend personalized content, while GANs are creating new frontiers in art and music generation.

The Future: A Horizon of Possibilities

As neural networks and deep learning continue to evolve, we're only scratching the surface of their potential. Imagine AI systems capable of developing new drugs, predicting and mitigating natural disasters, or even helping us decipher ancient lost languages.

However, with great power comes great responsibility. It is crucial that we continue to develop these technologies ethically and responsibly, ensuring that they benefit all of humanity.

C# example for facial recognition

In this example, we will not use the ML.Net library, but rather Emgu.CV, which is one of the most popular libraries for image processing and computer vision, which are areas that have gained great relevance in modern applications, such as security, industrial automation and video analysis.

We will not create a model as it is something that depends on a large amount of images and training time to arrive at a minimally acceptable result, so we will use an already trained model as the idea is to demonstrate how to use the tools in C#.

What is Emgu.CV?

OpenCV (Open Source Computer Vision Library) is a widely used open-source library for image processing and computer vision. It provides a range of functionalities for image analysis, object detection, facial recognition, video manipulation, machine learning, and more. It is written primarily in C++ and has bindings for other languages, such as Python, Java, and C#.

Emgu CV is a wrapper for OpenCV that allows developers to use OpenCV in the .NET environment (C#, VB.NET, F#). It encapsulates OpenCV functionality into classes and methods that can be used directly from C#.

A wrapper is an abstraction layer that wraps another library or code to make it easier to use in different languages or environments. Emgu CV is a wrapper because:

- **Provides bindings for OpenCV** : It exposes OpenCV functions in a more friendly way for the .NET environment, making the use of the library more intuitive.

- **It uses OpenCV as a base** : Emgu CV does not implement computer vision algorithms on its own, but only makes those from OpenCV available for use in .NET.

- **Facilitates interoperability** : OpenCV is written in C++, and Emgu CV provides a way to use it in C# and .NET without having to write C++ code directly.

- **Manages pointers and native calls** : Since OpenCV uses pointers and low-level data structures, Emgu CV converts these elements to .NET managed objects.

-

Main features of Emgu.CV

The library offers several features, including:

- **Image processing** : Application of filters, edge detection, color transformation, among others.

- **Object detection and facial recognition** : Algorithms such as Haar Cascade and neural networks for face identification.

- **Real-time video processing** : Capture video from webcams and IP cameras.

- **Pattern recognition** : Shape identification, barcode reading and OCR (Optical Character Recognition).

- **Machine learning integration** : Ability to use trained models for advanced image recognition.

C# Example of Installation and Execution

** This project is also available at https://github.com/wagnersalvi/LivroMaquinas for download including the model

Requirements:

- Visual Studio 2022 with .Net Core 8 installed

- Camera of at least 720p (below may not have enough resolution)

- Emgu.CV Library (Download via Nuget)

- Download a trained facial recognition model from https://github.com/opencv/opencv/tree/master/data/haarc ascades

Haar Cascade

The haarcascade_frontalface_default.xml file is a cascade classifier based on the Haar Cascade algorithm for frontal face detection. It is part of the pre-trained models provided by OpenCV and is widely used for face recognition in computer vision applications.

How does it work?

The Haar Cascade algorithm was developed by Paul Viola and Michael Jones and works by training on thousands of positive (with faces) and negative (without faces) images. It uses sliding windows to analyze different parts of the image and identify patterns that correspond to a face.

The trained model is stored in XML format, containing the coefficients required for detection.

Within the mentioned link we have several pre-trained models, and you can find several, such as models that evaluate not only the face but the whole body, whether or not the person is wearing glasses, using a mask, etc.

Step by step:

- Creating a WPF project within Visual Studio 2022

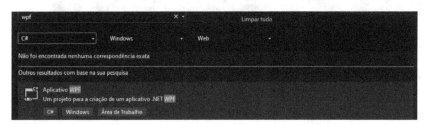

- Installing the Emgu.CV and Emgu.CV.runtime.windows Packages

- Download the haarcascade_frontalface_default.xml file from https://github.com/opencv/opencv/tree/master/data/haarc ascades . The file is a cascade classifier based on the Haar Cascade algorithm for frontal face detection. It is part of the pre-trained models provided by OpenCV and is widely used for face recognition in computer vision applications.

XAML code

In the XAML file, copy the code below, which only has one image component where the video will be demonstrated.

```xml
<Window
    x:Class="WpfApp2.MainWindow"
    xmlns="http://schemas.microsoft.com/winfx/2006/xaml/presentation"
    xmlns:x="http://schemas.microsoft.com/winfx/2006/xaml"
    xmlns:d="http://schemas.microsoft.com/expression/blend/2008"
    xmlns:mc="http://schemas.openxmlformats.org/markup-compatibility/2006"
    Title="Reconhecimento de Face em C#"
    Width="800"
    Height="450"
    Closing="MainWindow_OnClosing"
    mc:Ignorable="d">
    <Grid>
        <Image
            x:Name="cameraImage"
            HorizontalAlignment="Stretch"
            VerticalAlignment="Stretch" />
    </Grid>
</Window>
```

C# Code

Creating some variables that will be used to control the camera

```
private VideoCapture capture;
private CascadeClassifier faceCascade;
private bool isRunning = false;
private DispatcherTimer timer;
```

In the window constructor class we will have the code below where it will load the model and create a timer to capture the image from the camera every 30 milliseconds.

```
0 referências
public MainWindow()
{
    InitializeComponent();

    try
    {
        // Inicializa a captura de vídeo (câmera padrão)
        capture = new VideoCapture();

        // Carrega o classificador Haar Cascade para detecção facial
        faceCascade = new CascadeClassifier("haarcascade_frontalface_default.xml"); // Certifique-se de ter o arquivo XML

        // Inicializa o timer para atualizar a imagem
        timer = new DispatcherTimer();
        timer.Tick += ProcessFrame;
        timer.Interval = TimeSpan.FromMilliseconds(30); // Ajuste conforme necessário
        timer.Start();

        isRunning = true;
    }
    catch (Exception ex)
    {
        MessageBox.Show($"Erro ao inicializar: {ex.Message}");
    }
}
```

A method to stop the camera when closing the application

```
2 referências
private void StopCapture()
{
    if (timer != null)
    {
        timer.Stop();
        timer = null;
    }
    if (capture != null)
    {
        capture.Stop();
        capture.Dispose();
        capture = null;
    }
    if (faceCascade != null)
    {
        faceCascade.Dispose();
        faceCascade = null;
    }
    isRunning = false;
}
```

And calling this method when closing the window

```
1 referência
private void MainWindow_OnClosing(object sender, System.ComponentModel.CancelEventArgs e)
{
    StopCapture();
}
```

And finally, the method that takes the camera frame and analyzes the image to assess whether or not there is a face in the image. If there is, it draws a green square around it.

```csharp
private void ProcessFrame(object sender, EventArgs e)
{
    if (!isRunning) return;

    try
    {
        Mat frame = capture.QueryFrame();
        if (frame == null) return;

        Image<Bgr, byte> image = frame.ToImage<Bgr, byte>();

        // Detecta rostos na imagem
        Rectangle[] faces = faceCascade.DetectMultiScale(
            image,
            1.1,
            10,
            System.Drawing.Size.Empty);

        // Desenha retângulos verdes ao redor dos rostos detectados
        foreach (Rectangle face in faces)
        {
            image.Draw(face, new Bgr(Color.Green), 2);
        }

        // Converte a imagem para um formato que WPF pode exibir
        Bitmap bitmap = new Bitmap(frame.Width, frame.Height, System.Drawing.Imaging.PixelFormat.Format24bppRgb);
        System.Drawing.Imaging.BitmapData bitmapData = bitmap.LockBits(new Rectangle(0, 0, frame.Width, frame.Height),
            System.Drawing.Imaging.ImageLockMode.WriteOnly, System.Drawing.Imaging.PixelFormat.Format24bppRgb);

        int imageSize = frame.Width * frame.Height * 3; // 3 bytes por pixel (B, G, R)
        byte[] data = new byte[imageSize];
        System.Runtime.InteropServices.Marshal.Copy(image.MIplImage.ImageData, data, 0, imageSize);
        System.Runtime.InteropServices.Marshal.Copy(data, 0, bitmapData.Scan0, imageSize);

        bitmap.UnlockBits(bitmapData);

        var bitmapSource = Imaging.CreateBitmapSourceFromHBitmap(
            bitmap.GetHbitmap(),
            IntPtr.Zero,
            Int32Rect.Empty,
            BitmapSizeOptions.FromEmptyOptions());

        // Exibe a imagem no controle Image da WPF
        cameraImage.Source = bitmapSource;
    }
    catch (Exception ex)
    {
        MessageBox.Show($"Erro ao processar frame: {ex.Message}");
        StopCapture(); // Para a captura em caso de erro
    }
}
```

Testing the application

In the image below we can see that it recognized my face and marked it within a green square and it can be tested with several people and even point to a photo with "n" people and it will recognize them, the better the camera the better the result will be.

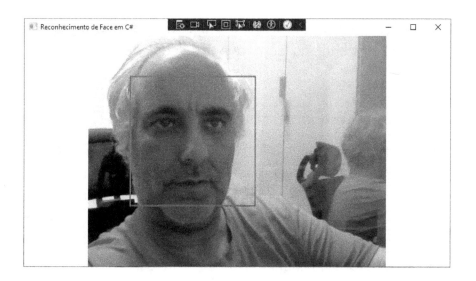

Chapter 9: Machine Learning Automation in C#

Machine Learning Automation Concept

In this chapter, we will explore the concept of Machine Learning (ML) automation and how it can be implemented in C# using the AutoML.NET tool. We will cover the definition and benefits of ML automation, and provide a practical example of using AutoML.NET in a C# project.

Machine learning automation refers to the process of systematizing the steps required to develop a machine learning model. This includes tasks such as data preprocessing, algorithm selection, hyperparameter tuning, model training, and validation. Automation aims to simplify the development of ML models, making it more accessible, efficient, and less prone to human error.

Benefits of Automation in ML:

- **Efficiency:** Significantly reduces the time required to test and validate different models and parameters.
- **Accessibility:** Allows people with less experience in data science to create effective models without deep technical knowledge.
- **Consistency:** Minimizes variability in results due to human error or suboptimal testing methods.
- **Scalability:** Makes it easy to run multiple experiments simultaneously or implement large-scale ML systems.

Introduction to AutoML.NET

AutoML.NET is a Microsoft-provided library for automating machine learning within the ML.NET framework. It is a powerful tool that enables C# developers to build machine learning models without requiring a deep understanding of data science. AutoML.NET automates algorithm selection and hyperparameter tuning, making the modeling process easier.

We'll see how AutoML.NET can make the process of creating predictive models easier by automating the complex steps of the machine learning process. With it, developers can focus more on applying models and less on the complex mechanics of creating them.

By the end of this exercise, you should have gained a solid understanding of how to integrate ML automation into your C# projects and how the AutoML.NET platform can be a powerful ally in developing effective data solutions.

Practical Example Using AutoML.NET

In this example, we will create a C# project that uses AutoML.NET to predict house prices based on a fictitious dataset that will initially have the same idea as our first house price prediction model.

Environment Preparation

Create a new C# Console App project in Visual Studio or any other development environment of your choice.

Add the following dependencies via NuGet: Microsoft.ML and Microsoft.ML.AutoML using the command:

```
dotnet add package Microsoft.ML
dotnet add package Microsoft.ML.AutoML
```

Source Code:

We will use the same PropertyData model used in the initial example of the book.

```csharp
public class DadosImovel
{
    3 referências
    public float Tamanho { get; set; }
    2 referências
    public float Preco { get; set; }
}

1 referência
public class PredicaoImovel
{
    [ColumnName("Score")]
    1 referência
    public float PrecoPrevisao { get; set; }
}
```

And finally the code below

```csharp
0 referências
class Program
{
    0 referências
    static async Task Main(string[] args)
    {
        MLContext contextoML = new MLContext();
        //contextoML.Log += (sender, e) => Console.WriteLine(e.Message);

        // Importar ou criar dados de treinamento
        var rand = new Random();
        var dadosCasas = new List<DadosImovel>();

        for (int i = 0; i < 100; i++)
        {
            // Gerar um tamanho entre 50 e 500m²
            float tamanho = (float)(rand.NextDouble() * 450 + 50);
            // Definir preço como uma função do tamanho com uma variação aleatória
            // Aqui, preço é aproximadamente tamanho * 0.8 com uma variação aleatória
            float preco = tamanho * 0.8f + (float)(rand.NextDouble() * 10 - 5);

            dadosCasas.Add(new DadosImovel { Tamanho = tamanho, Preco = preco });
        }

        // Imprimir os dados gerados (opcional)
        foreach (var dados in dadosCasas)
        {
            Console.WriteLine($"Tamanho: {dados.Tamanho:F1}, Preço: {dados.Preco:F1}");
        }
        IDataView dadosTreinamento = contextoML.Data.LoadFromEnumerable(dadosCasas);

        // Definir tarefa de regressão
        var experiment = contextoML.Auto().CreateRegressionExperiment(maxExperimentTimeInSeconds: 60);

        // Configurar treinamento
        var result = experiment.Execute(dadosTreinamento, labelColumnName: "Preco");

        // Avaliar o modelo
        Console.WriteLine($"Melhor modelo: {result.BestRun.TrainerName}");
        Console.WriteLine($"R-squared: {result.BestRun.ValidationMetrics.RSquared}");

        // Fazer predições
        var model = result.BestRun.Model;
        var input = new DadosImovel { Tamanho = 150.0F };
        var predictionFunction = contextoML.Model.CreatePredictionEngine<DadosImovel, PredicaoImovel>(model);
        var prediction = predictionFunction.Predict(input);

        Console.WriteLine($"Preço previsto: {prediction.PrecoPrevisao}");
    }
}
```

Result

```
Tamanho: 193,5, Preço: 151,3
Tamanho: 78,7, Preço: 59,5
Tamanho: 358,4, Preço: 286,9
Melhor modelo: ReplaceMissingValues=>Concatenate=>FastForestRegression
R-squared: 0,9337421519816982
Preço previsto: 123,14584
```

Code Explanation

Data Structure Definition:

- We create a PropertyData class that contains properties for Size and Price. This represents each entry in our dataset.

Program Initialization

- Inside the Main method, we start by creating a list to store our data (List<DadosImovel>) and a Random object to generate random numbers, simulating variation in the data.

Data Generation

- We use a for loop to create 100 instances of PropertyData.
  - Size: We generate a random size for each property between 50m^2 and 500m^2.
  - Price: We calculate the price as 80% of the size, adding a small random variation to reflect realistic fluctuations in the market.

Storage and Printing

- Each size and price pair generated is added to the dataHouses list. Finally, the program prints the generated data, so that we can visualize the characteristics of each property.

Machine Learning Ready

- The generated list (dadosCasas) is ready to be converted into a format usable in ML.NET (IDataView), allowing this data to be used for training machine learning models.

Chapter 10: Deploying and Maintaining ML Models in C#

Deploying and maintaining Machine Learning (ML) models are crucial steps in the lifecycle of an ML project. After training and evaluating a model, it must be deployed to a production environment so that it can be used by end users. Additionally, it is essential to keep the model up-to-date and adjusted to changes in the data and environment to ensure its continued effectiveness.

Basic Concepts

Before diving into the details of deploying and maintaining C# ML models, it is important to understand a few basic concepts:

- Deployment: This is the process of putting an ML model into production, making it accessible to end users.
- Maintenance: This is the process of updating and adjusting an ML model to ensure its continued effectiveness.
- ML model: An algorithm trained on data to perform a specific task, such as classification or regression.

Challenges of Deploying and Maintaining ML Models

Deploying and maintaining ML models in C# can be challenging due to several factors, such as:

- Model complexity: Complex ML models can be difficult to deploy and maintain, especially if they are developed in different programming languages.
- Integration with existing systems: ML models need to be integrated with existing systems, which can be challenging, especially if the systems are built on different technologies.
- Data refresh: ML models need to be refreshed regularly to ensure their continued effectiveness, which can be challenging, especially if the data is large and complex.
- Monitoring and tuning: MLam models need to be monitored and tuned regularly to ensure their continued effectiveness, which can be challenging, especially if the models are complex.

Deploying ML Models in C#

Deploying ML models in C# can be done in a number of ways, including:

- Using ML libraries: ML libraries like ML.NET and Accord.NET provide tools and resources for deploying ML models in C#.
- Using cloud services: Cloud services like Azure Machine Learning and Google Cloud AI Platform provide tools and capabilities for building ML models in C#.
- Using containers: Containers like Docker provide a way to deploy C# ML models in an isolated and scalable way.

Maintaining ML Models in C#

Maintaining ML models in C# can be done in a number of ways, including:

- Data refresh: refresh the data used to train the model to ensure its continued effectiveness.
- Hyperparameter tuning: Adjust the model's hyperparameters to ensure its continued effectiveness.
- Performance monitoring: Monitor model performance to ensure its continued effectiveness.

Monitoring and Updating Models in C#

When developing Machine Learning applications in C#, deploying a model is not the end of the process. To ensure the efficiency and accuracy of predictions over time, it is essential to monitor the model's performance and update it when necessary.

In this chapter, we will explore strategies for monitoring and updating Machine Learning models using ML.NET, including metrics collection, data drift detection, and dynamic retraining.

Model Performance Monitoring

A model's accuracy can degrade over time due to changing patterns in the data. Monitoring performance ensures that the model remains relevant. Some common metrics to monitor include:

- **Accuracy** : Measures the proportion of correct predictions.
- **& Recall** : Essential for classification.

- **Mean Squared Error** (MSE) and **Mean Absolute Error** (MAE): Error indicators in regression models.

- **AUC-ROC** : Measures the quality of binary classification.

Data Drift Detection

Changes in input data can compromise model quality. Some approaches to detect drift include:

- Compare distribution of new and old data.
- Monitor unexpected forecasts.
- Create an alert when metrics fall below a threshold.

Model Update and Retraining

When we detect a loss of performance, we can retrain the model with new data. ML.NET makes this process easier through the Fit command.

Implementing a Continuous Pipeline

To make the process automatic, we can:

- Collect forecasts and calculate metrics.
- Compare with previous metrics.
- Trigger a retraining if necessary.
- Update the deployed model.

Frameworks like Azure Machine Learning and MLFlow can help with automation.

Chapter 11: Ethics and Responsibility in Machine Learning

Machine learning has the power to transform the way we make decisions, automate processes, and interact with technology. But like any great tool, it comes with great responsibilities. In this chapter, we'll explore three fundamental aspects of ML ethics: bias and fairness, data privacy and security, and model interpretability. Understanding these concepts is essential to ensuring that we create models that are not only efficient, but also fair and trustworthy.

Bias and Fairness in ML Models

Imagine an artificial intelligence system used to decide whether someone is eligible for a bank loan. Now imagine that this model was trained on historical data that reflects past discrimination. What happens? The system could continue to perpetuate injustices!

How Does Bias Arise?

Bias occurs when a model learns unfair patterns present in the data. This can happen for several reasons:

- **Imbalanced data** : If a model is trained mostly on information from a specific group, it may have difficulty generalizing to other groups.

- **Misdefining the problem** : If the model's evaluation metric prioritizes one group over another, it can reinforce inequalities.

- **Misinterpretation of data** : If a model assumes that certain features determine an outcome, without considering the context, it may be biased.

How to Ensure Fairness?

Here are some best practices for making models fairer:

- **Analyze the distribution of training data** to verify that there is adequate representation of all groups.

- **Test the model's performance for different subgroups** and ensure there are no disparities.

- **Apply bias mitigation techniques** , such as resampling the data or adjusting the forecasts.

Tools like Fairlearn (Microsoft) and AI Fairness 360 (IBM) help detect and reduce bias in ML models.

Privacy and Data Security

Machine Learning models depend on large volumes of data, but with this comes a big challenge: how to ensure that this data is protected?

Risks Involved

- **Leakage of sensitive information** : A model may memorize sensitive data and end up leaking that information.

- **Adversarial attacks** : Malicious actors can manipulate input data to trick the model and change its predictions.

- **Data misuse** : If data is not properly anonymized, third parties may be able to identify individuals from the model's predictions.

How to Protect Data?

- **Anonymization** : Remove information that can identify individuals.

- **Encryption** : Ensure that data in transit and at rest is protected.

- **Federated training** : An approach that allows you to train models without transferring data to a central server.

- **Audit and compliance** : Ensure that the system follows regulations such as **LGPD (Brazil)** and **GDPR (Europe)** .

When building ML solutions, it's important to think about security from the start. Measures like access control, logging, and auditing can make all the difference!

Model Interpretability

One of the biggest challenges in machine learning is the ability to explain how and why a model arrived at a particular prediction.

This is essential in areas such as healthcare and finance, where decisions need to be justified.

Models as "Black Boxes"

More complex algorithms, such as deep neural networks, can be difficult to interpret. This can lead to problems such as:

- **Lack of trust** : Users may not trust models they cannot understand.

- **Difficulty detecting errors** : If a model makes an error, it can be difficult to figure out why.

- **Legal and ethical issues** : Regulations require that automated decisions can be explained.

How to Make Models More Interpretable?

Fortunately, there are approaches to increasing transparency:

- **Simpler models** : Whenever possible, opt for more interpretable models, such as decision trees and linear regression.

- **Interpretability techniques** :

  - **SHAP (Shapley Additive Explanations)** : Helps to understand the contribution of each variable in the forecast.

  - **LIME (Local Interpretable Model-Agnostic Explanations)** : Generates local explanations to predict how the model behaves in specific cases.

- **Visualizations** : Tools like the Azure **ML Dashboard can help you explore how your model makes decisions.**

Having an interpretable model does not mean giving up accuracy. The important thing is to find a balance between performance and understandability!

Chapter 12: Case Studies and Practical Projects in Machine Learning

Learning Machine Learning in theory is essential, but there's no substitute for practice! In this chapter, we explore three real-world applications of ML in C#, with projects that can be implemented to solidify your knowledge. Let's dive into the following case studies:

- Predictive analysis of customer churn
- Fraud detection in financial transactions
- Product demand forecast

Each of these projects addresses common challenges faced by businesses and how we can solve them with ML.NET.

Predictive Analysis of Customer Cancellation

The Problem

Businesses rely on customer retention to maintain revenue. Customer churn can be reduced if we know in advance who is likely to leave and take steps to prevent it.

Solution with ML.NET

We can train a classification model that predicts the likelihood of a customer churning based on their usage history, which has the benefits of allowing the company to act before the customer leaves and helping define better retention strategies.

The model class would look something like this:

```
public class CustomerData
{
public float Active Months { get; set; }
public float Monthly Spending { get; set; }
public float Complaints { get; set; }
public bool Cancellation { get; set; }
}

public class PredicationCancellation
{
[ColumnName("PredictedLabel")]
public bool Predication { get; set; }
}
```

Fraud Detection in Financial Transactions

The Problem

Fraud in financial transactions causes huge losses for banks and consumers. The challenge is to identify suspicious transactions without blocking legitimate transactions.

Solution with ML.NET

We use a classification model to identify fraudulent patterns in transactions. The class would look something like this:

```
public class TransactionData
{
public float Value { get; set; }
public float Time { get; set; }
public float Location { get; set; }
public bool Fraud { get; set; }
}
```

Product Demand Forecasting

The Problem

Companies need to forecast product demand to avoid insufficient or excessive stocks.

Solution with ML.NET

We can use a regression model to predict future sales based on purchase history. The class would look something like this:

```
public class SalesData
{
public float Month { get; set; }
public floatQuantitySold { get; set; }
```

}